OCTOBER DEDICATIONS

OCTOBER DEDICATIONS
十月的献诗

Selected Poetry of
Mang Ke
芒克

Translated from Chinese by Lucas Klein,
Huang Yibing and Jonathan Stalling

Zephyr Press & The Chinese University Press of Hong Kong
Brookline, Mass | Hong Kong

Cover image by Xu Bing
Book design by typeslowly
Printed in Hong Kong

"Street," "Even After Death We Grow Old," and "Late Years" appeared in the March 2016
issue of *Cha: An Asian Literary Journal* (Issue 31). "Dedications: 1972–1973," "Sunlight,"
and "Lamp" appeared in the January 2015 issue of *Asymptote*. "Sky" and "Sunflower in the Sun"
appeared in the anthology *Push Open the Window* (Copper Canyon Press, 2011).

This publication is supported by the Jintian Literary Foundation.
Zephyr Press also acknowledges with gratitude the financial support
of the Massachusetts Cultural Council.

masscentral council.org

Zephyr Press, a non-profit arts and education 501(c)(3) organization,
publishes literary titles that foster a deeper understanding of cultures
and languages. Zephyr Press books are distributed to the trade in the U.S.
and Canada by Consortium Book Sales and Distribution [www.cbsd.com].

Published for the rest of the world by:
The Chinese University Press
The Chinese University of Hong Kong
Sha Tin, N.T., Hong Kong

Cataloguing-in publication data is available from the Library of Congress.

ZEPHYR PRESS
www.zephyrpress.org

JINTIAN
www.jintian.net

THE CHINESE UNIVERSITY PRESS
www.chineseupress.com

CONTENTS

Translator's Foreword

In a poem about visiting an open-air market in the town of Baiyangdian, Xi Chuan 西川 writes,

> how bright the sun I do not know
> but I've seen the sun shine so an old man held the light in his eyes
>
> how many people the sun illuminates in this market I do not know
> but I've heard the sun make pots pans ladles spoons open their
> > mouths to speak

> 太阳有多亮我不知道
> 但太阳晃得老汉双眼含光我看到了
>
> 太阳照耀多少人聚在集市上我不知道
> 但太阳让锅碗瓢勺开口说话我听到了[1]

The title notes that Xi Chuan traveled with Mang Ke 芒克 to Baiyangdian, the lakeside town in Hebei province to which the latter poet had been "sent down" in 1969. But the sun here is different from that of Mang Ke's 1983 "Sunflower in the Sun" 阳光中的向日葵. For Xi Chuan the Baiyangdian sun is the sun, visible and accessible to the shoppers and shopkeepers in the countryside market in ways it might not have been to consumers and salespeople in Beijing. For Mang Ke, drawing on the iconography of the Cultural Revolution, in which the citizens of the People's Republic were drawn as sunflowers, basking in the light of their solar Chairman Mao, the sun is a dictatorial force, threatening not nourishment but strangulation— against which the sunflower stands in open opposition:

do you see
do you see that sunflower in the sun
you see, it doesn't bow its head
but turns it back
it turns its head
as if to bite through
the rope around its neck
held by the sun's hands

你看到了吗
你看到阳光中的那棵向日葵了吗
你看它，它没有低下头
而是把头转向身后
就好象是为了一口咬断
那套在它脖子上的
那牵在太阳手中的绳索

One of Mang Ke's most overtly political poems—certainly the most unequivocal in this collection—"Sunflower in the Sun" presents a good starting place for understanding his trajectory as a poet and his development of contemporary poetry in mainland China, as the sunflower marks the point when the implicit politics of the poet's language becomes most explicit.

Before he was known as Mang Ke, the Beijing-born Jiang Shiwei 姜世伟 (b. 1950) followed Chairman Mao's Cultural Revolution call for educated youths to "rusticate," or be sent down to the countryside, to learn revolution and proper socialist behavior from the peasants. While the extent to which he learned socialism is unclear, he did develop the framework of a style that would transform into contemporary Chinese poetry. Together with Duo Duo 多多 (penname of Li Shizheng 栗世征, b. 1951) and the poet Genzi 根子 (penname of Yue Caigen 岳彩根, later known as Yue Zhong 岳重, b. 1951), they would become known as the

"Three Musketeers of Baiyangdian" 白洋淀三剑客. In what is still the best early history of contemporary poetry as it grew in the sixties and seventies, Maghiel van Crevel writes that "Mang Ke was the first to develop an individual and mature mode of expression in Experimental poetry written in and around Beijing in the early 1970s," and defines his style as one of "simple vocabulary, precise and sometimes repetitive wording, and a limited number of recurring images":

> In a blend of common sense and fantasy, powers of Nature such as day and night, the sun and the wind, are personified and endowed with human or animal attributes like eyes, hair or the ability to cry. They have ambiguous but intimate relationships with the protagonists, usually denoted by personal pronouns. In free verse with inconspicuous but frequent rhyme and rhythm, his poetry is distinguished by its flowing diction more than anything else. Together, these features make for a sophisticated naivete in his poetic oeuvre.[2]

It is from this naïve sophistication of intimate ambiguity within flowing diction that contemporary Chinese poetry originated.

While Mang Ke's early poems read today with an undeniable sophistication, this should not override the innocence van Crevel notes, or their basis in simple, straightforward play. Because of his cavalier attitude and wildness in Baiyangdian, his friends called him *Houzi* 猴子, or Monkey, and when I asked Mang Ke to explain a line from one of his earlier poems so I could translate it better, he told me that in those days they were just writing for fun, so I shouldn't take it too seriously.

But within this fun, a focus on the minute reveals a language of political significance. In their study of the changes to the Chinese language during the Cultural Revolution, Lowell Dittmer and Chen Ruoxi refer to what they call the "inflation of language." Against popular slogans of the day like "Hold high the great red banner of Mao Zedong Thought to wage the Great Proletarian Cultural Revolution to the end" 高举毛泽东思想伟大红旗把无产阶级文化大革命进行到底, the lines of Mang Ke

> in the center of the sky
> hangs a strand of sunlight-softened hair
> the city
> saturated in eastern luxury

> 当天空中
> 垂下了一缕阳光柔软的头发
> 城市
> 浸透了东方的豪华

must have been read as shockingly direct and heterodox at the time. The sunlight represents not Mao Zedong, but is rather, as with Xi Chuan's poem, just the sunlight. If Dittmer and Chen are correct, that written Chinese had once been known "for its subtlety and delicacy, for . . . honesty and sincerity, moderation and respect for wisdom, and also for its cultivation of a refined and elegant literary style," then Mang Ke's telegraphic, imagist writing represents a return to an earlier standard of subtlety and sincerity. Likewise, if the Cultural Revolution's "monothematic emphasis on politics deprived the language of subtlety by polarizing alternatives and reducing the vocabulary to a terminology of warfare," then the popularity and power of Mang Ke's poetry may have come from the heterodox interpretive space it opens in its understated—and anti-inflationary—use of language.[3]

In its understatement, Mang Ke's writing takes an early stance against what Chinese critic Li Tuo has called *Mao wenti* 毛文体, translated as "Mao style" or "Maospeak."[4] Mang Ke's implicitly counter-Maoist poetics not only grew into the explicit politics of "Sunflower in the Sun," but also into a poetry movement with its own publication mechanism, the first non-official literary journal in the history of the People's Republic of China—where publishing was strictly a state-controlled affair. Back in Beijing, Mang Ke co-founded, with another young poet named Zhao Zhenkai 赵振开 (b. 1949), the journal *Jintian* 今天 (*Today*), to publish poetry, fiction, and criticism that would offer new forms of literary expression in a China emerging from the Cultural Revolution. Securing a printing press for a private venue was a crime in those days, but the editors rode their bicycles (with covered license plates) to deliver their issues to the steps of bureau buildings and official organizations. Still, they used pseudonyms for protection: Zhao was given the name Bei Dao 北岛, and he gave Jiang Shiwei the name Mang Ke in turn—as it sounded like the English word "Monkey," his earlier nickname in Baiyangdian.

Jintian ran from 1978 to 1980, publishing nine bi-monthly issues and seven series titles, distributing a total of nearly twenty thousand copies to readers in Beijing and throughout China. Bei Dao recalls that their literary salons were the largest Beijing has ever known, and their public poetry readings attracted audiences in the hundreds. Not surprisingly, *Jintian* was shut down, and the government launched an official campaign against writing it called *menglong* 朦胧, or "obscure" (often mistranslated as "misty"). Bei Dao re-launched the magazine in exile after 1989. Although *Jintian* is not officially available in mainland China, it is widely read there, and remains one of the most important journals of contemporary Chinese literature and thought, with an influential website and an international publishing mission to promote contemporary Chinese poetry. *Jintian* has always been not only independent but often oppositional, and there is a much larger non-official discourse on poetry in China today. As such, poetry maintains an association with counter-hegemonic principles and political opposition—in contrast to fiction, which publishes in official venues and is often targeted at filmmakers.

This assumption of political opposition has come at significant cost to a large number of poets, and many were in exile for years. Though Mang Ke has always lived in Beijing, one journalist writes that, in the aftermath of the Tiananmen Square massacre on June 4, 1989, because his name was on a petition calling for the release of human rights activist Wei Jingsheng 魏京生, Mang Ke "was detained at his home. A black bag was placed over his head and he was taken to a place he didn't know. After two days, he was released. The people who took him said he was detained for his own safety."[5] Over the years, Mang Ke has devoted himself less to poetry than to painting—colorful abstracts that resemble but cannot be reduced to landscapes—but I do not think this represents a turn away from the implicit politics of being a poet. He has also published a novel of frank sexuality and Cultural Revolution micro-histories, *Wild Things* 野事 (1994), which Wendy Larson, in her study of *Freud and Revolutionary Spirit in 20th Century China*, says "deconstructs the very notion of spiritual embodiment and consciousness through his spatial flattening and oddly disconnected histories, events, and styles."[6] What links these efforts is a continued focus on the luminous detail as a way of speaking against the prevailing ethos of overly or wrongly politicized language.

The final pieces in this book are from Mang Ke's latest major poem, "Time Without Time" 沒有时间的时间. No longer writing against linguistic inflation, "Time Without Time" begins in the absence of any sun or light:

there are no more feelings growing here
it is a blank expanse of time here
dark and cold
solitary and empty

这里已不再有感情生长
这里是一片光秃秃的时间
阴暗而又寒冷
寂静而又空荡

The poem runs to sixty pages in Chinese; hence, it is being excerpted here. While the sun in Mang Ke's earliest works was simply the sun, and later became a menacing dictator referring to, but also refracting the earlier depiction of Mao, here its absence shines a critique on the destitution of a society on the verge of believing in nothing. That this poem was written in the late eighties—a time in China many look back to nostalgically as a decade not only of reform and opening up but also of internationalist intellectual optimism—underscores the poet's insightful darkness.

Pushing back through this darkness, we might again glimpse Baiyangdian. Though I remarked earlier that in Xi Chuan's poem, as in Mang Ke's earliest works, the sun is the sun, this is not to say that Xi Chuan believes Baiyangdian to be any kind of cultural or economic holdover:

> the waters of Baiyangdian grow gradually smaller under the sun
> a hero from the Anti-Japanese War still living today gets rolled
> into the market economy's great wave

白洋淀的水域在太阳下渐渐缩小
有抗日老英雄一直活到今朝卷入市场经济的大潮

Nevertheless, the economic and social reality Xi Chuan represents, and whose problems he handles, is distinct from that of the society to which Mang Ke's poems are addressed. And yet there is a line from one to the other, and along that line a similarity, a continuity. Today's poet addresses the inexorability of the market and writes against it; yesterday's poet writes against language inflation and the over-politicization that forecasted economic inflation. But this is not to relegate Mang Ke only to the yesterday, as both in his founding of *Jintian* and in the focus on clear detail in his earliest works, he has effectively created the possibility of poetry in China even now. In that, he remains a poet of today, and the light of his sun still shines.

★ ★ ★

Translating Mang Ke's poetry my goal has been, as always, to reflect not only what the poems say in Chinese but how they say it. Fortunately, a tradition of modern poetry in English also has focused on direct presentation of the luminous detail as a means of countering linguistic inflation, just as in Mang Ke, and my translations tack toward this tradition. In an early draft of "Dusk," for instance, I had,

> by now it is dusk
> by now the dusk is like a
> stripped off
> and wind-dried animal hide

> 这时正是黄昏
> 这时的黄昏就象是一张
> 已被剥下来的
> 已被风干的兽皮一样

which I amended to,

> now is dusk
> the dusk now like
> a skinned-off
> wind-dried animal pelt

and then,

> now is dusk
> the dusk now like a
> skinned-off
> wind-dried animal pelt

before finally arriving at,

> now it is dusk
> the dusk now like
> a skinned
> wind-dried animal pelt

Amidst such concentration, Mang Ke's repetitions are important to get right. Like the persistent *zheli* 这里 in "Time Without Time," the recurrent *zheshi* 这时 in this poem places his work in the here and now. That explains part of my preference for "now," which grounds the poem more, I think, than my earlier "by now." I also feel that the English rhythm requires more variation as it establishes its theme than the Chinese does, where the repeated syllables can occur in the same spot in successive lines. And while I want to respect and recreate his economy, I also want to draw attention to the language only where Mang Ke himself does, as well—hence my addition of a syllable in "now it is dusk," over "now is dusk." The lines can afford this word, I think, because of the reduction of "by now the dusk is like" to "the dusk now like," and "skinned-off" to "skinned." Overall, a progression of paring down and simplification.

I find the same aims and methods in the translations of Mang Ke by Yibing Huang and Jonathan Stalling, published in the anthology *Push Open the Window* (Copper Canyon, 2011), and so I have included some of their work in this volume as well, with minor edits for stylistic consistency.

Along with Mang Ke, my thanks go to Bei Dao, Christopher Mattison, Wang Ling, Simon Patton, Maghiel van Crevel, Eleanor Goodman, Ma Anting, and above all my wife, Shenxin Li, without whom this book would not have been possible.

—Lucas Klein, Hong Kong

Endnotes

1. Xi Chuan 西川, "Feelings in the Baiyangdian Open-Air Market with Mang Ke and Others. July, 2004" 与芒克等同游白洋淀集市有感. 2004年7月, *Gou Yimeng* 够一梦 [A Dream's Worth], *Xinlu Shicong* (Chongqing: Zhongqing daxue chubanshe, 2013), 168–170.

2. Maghiel van Crevel, *Language Shattered: Contemporary Chinese Poetry and Duoduo*, CNWS Publications, vol. 38 (Leiden, The Netherlands: Research School CNWS, 1996), 46. For more, see van Crevel, 46–50. As for the "Three Musketeers" appellation, van Crevel notes that "the invention of the Baiyangdian School of Poetry may amount to no more than the observation that among Beijing's early Experimental poets were three classmates who had moved to the same village and all wrote poetry, or to no more than a joke that later began to lead a life of its own," 50.

3. Lowell Dittmer and Chen Ruoxi 陳若曦, *Ethics and Rhetoric of the Chinese Cultural Revolution* (Center for Chinese Studies, Institute of East Asian Studies, University of California, 1981), 108.

4. Li Tuo 李陀 developed this influential notion over a number of essays written in the eighties and nineties. For a representative look in English, see "The New Vitality of Modern Chinese," in *Inside Out: Modernism and Postmodernism in Chinese Literary Culture*, ed. Wendy Larson and Anne Wedell-Wedellsborg (Aarhus: Aarhus University Press, 1993), 65–77; and "Resisting Writing," in *Politics, Ideology, and Literary Discourse in Modern China: Theoretical Interventions and Cultural Critique*, ed. Kang Liu and Xiaobing Tang, trans. Mary Scoggin (Durham: Duke University Press, 1993), 273–277. Li Tuo and other critics tend to use this term in reference to prose fiction, but for an analysis focusing on poetry, see Simon Patton, "Notes Toward a Nomad Subjectivity: The Poetics of Gu Cheng (1956–1993)," *Social Semiotics* 9, no. 1 (1999): 49–66.

5. Li Xuewen, "That Year, These Years: Stories of Tiananmen," trans. Little Bluegill, *China Digital Times*, June 25, 2012, http://chinadigitaltimes.net/2012/06/that-year-these-years-stories-tiananmen/. For the Chinese, see Li Xuewen 黎学文, "Na yinian, zhexie nian: yu liusi youguan de gushi" 那一年，这些年：与六四有关的故事

[That Year, These Years: Stories of Tiananmen], China Digital Times, June 9, 2012, http://chinadigitaltimes.net/chinese/2012/06/那一年，这些年：与六四有关的故事/.

6. Wendy Larson, *From Ah Q to Lei Feng: Freud and Revolutionary Spirit in 20th Century China* (Stanford: Stanford University Press, 2009), 118–119. See 118–132.

OCTOBER DEDICATIONS

十月的献诗

葡萄园

　一小块葡萄园
是我发甜的家

当秋风突然走进哐哐作响的门口
我的家园都是含着眼泪的葡萄

那使院子早早暗下来的墙头
有几只鸽子惊慌飞走

胆怯的孩子把弄脏的小脸
偷偷地藏在房后

平时总是在这里转悠的狗
这会儿不知溜到哪里去了

一群红色的鸡满院子扑腾
咯咯地叫个不休

我眼看着葡萄掉在地上
血在落叶中间流

这真是个想安宁也不得安宁的日子
这是在我家失去阳光的时候

The Vineyard

a small vineyard
is my sweetened home

when autumn winds rush past the rattling gate
my home is grapes with tears in their eyes

a few pigeons have been startled from
the wall that darkens the yard early

the cowardly child hides his dirty face
behind the house

the dog that usually hangs around
has gone off who knows where

a brood of red chickens tramples through the yard
with their endless clucking

I see grapes on the ground
blood flowing in fallen leaves

this is a day that cannot find peace
the day sunlight was lost from my home

城市

1

醒来
是你孤零零的脑袋
夜深了
风还在街上
像个迷路的孩子
东奔西撞

2

街
被折磨得
软弱无力地躺着
而流着唾液的大黑猫
饥饿地哭叫

3

这城市痛苦得东倒西歪
在黑暗中显得苍白

4

沉睡的天
你的头发被黑夜揉得凌乱
我被你搅得
彻夜不眠

City

wake
it's your lonesome head
late at night
the wind's still on the streets
like a lost child
clamoring about

streets
lying listlessly
in torment
that drooling black cat
cries in hunger

this city is askew with pain
seeming pale in the darkness

the sleeping sky
your hair mussed by night
you've disturbed me
past sleep

也许是梦
猜透了我的心情
才来替我抒情
啊，那被你欺骗着的
数不清的眼睛

5
当天空中
垂下了一缕阳光柔软的头发
城市
浸透了东方的豪华

6
人们在互相追逐
给后代留下颜色
孩子们从阳光里归来
给母亲带回爱

7
啊，城市
你这东方的孩子
在母亲干瘪的胸脯上
你寻找着粮食

maybe it's dreams
that gauge my emotions
before lyricizing for me
oh, those countless eyes
you lie to

5

in the center of the sky
hangs a strand of sunlight-softened hair
the city
saturated in eastern luxury

6

people pursuing each other
leave colors for their descendants
children returning from the sunlight
bring back love for their mothers

7

oh, city
child of the east
on mother's wizened breast
you seek grain

8

这多病的孩子对着你出神
太阳的七弦琴
你映出得却是她瘦弱的身影

9

城市啊
面对着饥饿的孩子睁大的眼睛
你却如此冰冷
如此无情

10

黑夜
总不愿意把我放过
它露着绿色的一只眼睛
可是
你什么也不对我说
夜深了
这天空似乎倾斜
我便安慰我
欢乐吧
欢乐是人人都会有的

8

this sickly child spellbound within you
the seven-stringed zither of the sun
what you reflect is her frail shadow

9

my city
your wide eyes in the face of starving children
you are that cold
that dispassionate

10

night
always unwilling to release me
shows a green eye
but
you say nothing to me
late at night
the sky's almost slanted
I console myself
be happy
happiness is what everyone can have

冻土地

像白云一样飘过去送葬的人群
河流缓慢地拖着太阳
长长的水面被染得金黄
多么寂静
多么辽阔
多么可怜的
那大片凋残的花朵

Frozen Land

pallbearers drift by like a cloud
the river slowly carries the sun
dying the water's long surface golden yellow
such stillness
such vastness
such sadness
a meadow of wilted flowers

秋天

1

果子熟了
这红色的血
我的果园
染红了同一块天空的夜晚

2

秋天
你这充满着情欲的日子
你的眼睛为什么暴露着我

3

在开花的时候
孩子们总要到田野里去做客
他们的欢乐
如今陪伴着耕种者
又走进这收割的季节
啊，秋天
我没有认错
你同样是开花的季节

Autumn

1

the fruit is ripe
this red blood
my orchard
reddening the same bit of night sky

2

autumn
your days full of passion
why do your eyes expose me

3

when flowers bloom
children will be guests in the meadow
their joy
accompanying plowmen
to enter the season of harvest
oh, autumn
I admit no wrong
you are also the season of flowering

4

你眼睛里的云朵
漫无目的地飘着
秋天呵
太阳为什么把你弄的这样瘦小

5

你怀中抱着的是什么
你寻找的是什么
那阳光下忧郁的人们
男人，女人，孩子，粮食
是一个家庭的需要
那就把摇篮里装满粮食

6

不要给孩子带来更多的眼泪
他们没有罪

7

带上那阳光中的一朵玫瑰红
把它献给爱情

4

the clouds in your eyes
drift aimlessly
but autumn
why has the sun made you so frail

5

what do you carry in your embrace
what are you seeking
those people under the sun
men, women, children, grain
are the needs of a family
so fill the cradles with grain

6

do not bring the children more tears
they are not guilty

7

bring over the red of the rose in the sun
bestow it to love

8

啊，秋天
你隐藏着多少颜色
黄昏，姑娘们浴后的毛巾
水波，戏弄着姑娘们的羞怯
夜，在疯狂地和女人纠缠着
秋天
秋天不逊色

9

秋天，我的生日过去了
你没有留下别的
也没有留下我
秋天
果子熟了
这红色的血

10

啊，你这蹲在门口的黑夜
我的寂寞
秋天来了
秋天什么也没有告诉我

8

oh, autumn
how many colors have you hidden
dusk, towels for bathing girls
ripples, toying with girls' timidity
night, madly entangling with women
autumn
autumn does not submit

9

autumn, my birthday has passed
you left nothing else
and didn't leave me, either
autumn
the fruit is ripe
this red blood

10

oh, night kneeling at the doorway
my silence
autumn is here
autumn has told me nothing

献诗：1972–1973

给生活

我时常去向山谷呼喊
当山谷送来了我的声音
我的声音
震动了我的心

给白洋淀

伟大的土地呵
你引起了我的激情

给太阳

你又一次地惊醒
你已满头花白

给诗人

你是飞向墓地的老鹰

Dedications: 1972–1973

For Life

sometimes I go shout in the valley
and when the valley sends back my voice
my voice
shocks my heart

For Baiyangdian

oh great land
you arouse my passions

For the Sun

once more you're awoken
hair gone salt and pepper

For a Poet

you are an eagle flying toward the graveyard

给一位姑娘

时间并不理会人性
但在匆忙的相遇中
她似乎也给我留下了温情

给夜晚

没有能使男人发昏的女人
也没有能使女人怀孕的男人

给小平的十八岁

在多病的孩子睁大的眼睛中
去理解美

给诗

那冷酷而又伟大的想象
是你，改造着
人类生活之外的荒凉

给人

只有地球便够了

For a Girl

time cannot comprehend humanity
but in a hurried encounter
she gave me something like warmth

For the Night

no woman to make a man giddy
and no man to make a woman pregnant

For Ping's 18th Year

in the wide eyes of the sickly child
go learn about beauty

For Poetry

the cold but great imagination
is you transforming
the desolation outside our lives

For Someone

only the world is enough

给朋友

这软弱无力的双手
将变成强有力的拳头

给冬天

生命
像火柴一样地点燃
为了温暖
为了燃烧
也为了烧完

给我的23岁生日

漂亮
健康
会思想

For a Friend

these powerless hands
become forceful fists

For Winter

life
lights like a match
to give warmth
to burn
and be burnt

For my 23rd Birthday

handsome
in health
full of thought

天空

1

太阳升起来
天空血淋淋的
犹如一块盾牌

2

日子像囚徒一样被放逐
没有人来问我
没有人宽恕我

3

我始终暴露着
只是把耻辱
用唾沫盖住

4

天空，天空
把你的疾病
从共和国的土地上扫除干净

Sky

1

the sun rises
the sky is blood-soaked
like a shield

2

days are banished like prisoners
no one comes to ask me
no one forgives me

3

I am always exposed
with only spit
to cover the shame

4

sky, sky
sweep the land of the Republic
free from your diseases

5

可是，希望变成了泪水
掉在地上
我们怎么能确保明天的人们不悲伤

6

我遥望着天空
我属于天空
天空呵
你提醒着
那向我走来的世界

7

为什么我在你的面前走过
总会感到羞怯
好像我老了
我拄着棍子
过去的青春终于落在我手中
我拄着棍子
天空
你要把我赶到哪里去
我为了你才这样力尽精疲

5

yet, hope turns to tears
falls to the ground
how can we make sure tomorrow's people won't feel sorrow

6

I look out into the sky
I belong to the sky
o sky
you remind me of
the world walking toward me

7

why am I always shy
when I pass in front of you
as if I were old
I lean on a cane
departed youth finally falls into my hand
I lean on a cane
sky
where are you leading me
I have exhausted myself only for you

8

谁不想把生活编织成花篮
可是，美好被打扫得干干净净
我们还年轻
你能否愉悦着我们的眼睛

9

带着你的温暖
带着你的爱
再用你的船
将我远载

10

希望
请你不要去得太远
你在我身边
就足以把我欺骗

11

太阳升起来
天空——这血淋淋的盾牌

8

who doesn't want to weave life into a flower basket
yet, beauty has been swept completely away
we are so young
can you enchant our eyes

9

bring your warmth
bring your love
and use your green boat
to carry me far away

10

hope
please don't go too far
stay by my side
and I will stay deceived

11

the sun rises
the sky—a blood-soaked shield

translated by Huang Yibing and Jonathan Stalling

路上的月亮

1

月亮陪着我走回家
我想把她带到将来的日子里去
一路静悄悄

2

咪，咪，咪
请你不要再把我打搅
你是人吗
也许你比人还可靠

3

当然了
没有比做人更值得骄傲
而你呢
你是猫
猫生下来就骚

4

我想把她带到将来的日子里去
不论怎样
想一想总比不想好

Moon on the Road

1

the moon walks home with me
I want to bring her into future days
silent along the way

2

mi, mi, mi
please don't bother me anymore
are you human
you may be even more reliable

3

of course
nothing merits pride more than human behavior
but you
you're a cat
and cats are nothing but trouble

4

I want to bring her into future days
no matter how
a bit of wanting is better than none

5

生活真是这样美好
睡觉

6

月亮独自在荒野上飘
她是什么时候失掉的
我一点儿也不知道

5

this is how beautiful life is
sleep

6

the moon hovers alone over the wilderness
when was she lost
I have no idea

十月的献诗

庄稼

秋天悄悄地来到我的脸上
我成熟了

劳动

我将和所有的马车一道
把太阳拉进麦田……

果实

多么可爱的孩子
多么可爱的目光
太阳像那树上的苹果
它下面是无数孩子奇妙的幻想

秋天的树林

没有你的眼睛
没有你的声音
地上落着红色的头巾

October Dedications

Crops

autumn silently appears on my face
I've matured

Labor

like all horse carts I will
pull the sun closer to the wheat field . . .

Fruit

such lovely children
such loving gazes
the sun is like the apple on a tree
beneath it are the fantasies of countless children

Autumn Forest

without your sight
without your voice
a red headscarf falls to the ground

遭遇

那是个像云片般飘动着的
女人的身影

小路

那在不停摇摆的白杨
那个背靠着白杨的姑娘
那条使姑娘失望的弯弯曲曲的路上……

风

我很想和你说
让我们并排走吧

云

我爱你
当你穿上那件白色的睡衣

河流

疲劳的人儿
你可愿意让我握住那只苍白的小手

Encounter

like a cloud floating by it was
a woman's shadow

Path

the white poplar ceaselessly swaying
the girl leaning against the poplar
the winding path that disappoints the girl . . .

Wind

what I want to say to you is
let's walk side by side

Cloud

I love you
when you wear those white pajamas

River

weary one
still you're happy to let me hold onto that little white hand

妻子

我将把所有的日子
都给你带去

土地

我全部的情感
都被太阳晒过

垦荒者

我是河流
我是奶浆
我要灌溉
我要哺养
我是铁犁
我是镰刀
我要耕种
我要收割

日落

太阳朝着没有人的地方走去了

Wife

I will bring all days
to you

Land

all my emotions
have been laid out in the sun

Land Reclaimer

I am the river
I am milk starch
I must irrigate
I must feed
I am the iron plow
I am the sickle
I must sow
I must reap

Sunset

the sun heads where no one is

孤独

小路，小路
我和你淹没在雾的深处

重逢

繁重的劳动
沉重的生活

浮冰

好一块白色的甲板
你可记得
在那里埋葬着往事和沉船

童年

那是一条我曾迷失过的道路

幸福

也许是
我生下来就为了爱你

Lonesomeness

path, little path
you and I drown in the depths of the fog

Reencounter

strenuous labor
burdensome life

Ice Floe

such white deck armor
you still remember
the past and shipwrecks buried there

Childhood

that's a road I got lost on once

Happiness

maybe it's
that I was born to love you

命运

最了解你的
就是你自己

自然

她是美丽的
她是大家的

遥望

过去的一切
可都是真的

夕阳

你想落在哪里
就请落在哪里吧

桅杆

只是挥手告别了落日
那只红肿的眼睛

Fate

the one who understands you most
is you

Nature

she is beautiful
she is everyone

Peering

all in the past
was true

Setting Sun

wherever you decide to go down
go down

Mast

just a wave goodbye to the sunset
that red and swollen eye

歌

对将来的抒情
仅仅是为了以往的罪过

孩子

那向我走来的黑夜对我说
你是我的

露宿

面对面的坐着
面对面的沉默
遍地是窝棚和火堆
遍地是散发着泥土味的男人的双腿

酒

那是座寂寞的小坟

田野

在她那孤零零的坟墓上写着：
我没有给你留下别的
我也没有给你留下我

Song

future lyricism
will only be for past crimes

Children

the night walking over said to me
you are mine

Sleeping Outdoors

sitting face to face
silently face to face
shacks and fire pits are all around
men's legs reaking of soil are all around

Liquor

it is a silent little grave

Field

on her lonely tombstone is written:
I left nothing else for you
I didn't even leave you me

生活

那早已为你准备好了痛苦与欢乐

路灯

整齐的光明
整齐的黑暗

回忆

你呀
这红红绿绿的夜
又不知该怎样地把我折磨

感情

猛地惊醒
便又爱上了寂寞

青春

在这里
在有着繁殖和生息的地方
我便被抛弃了

Life

the pain and joy already prepared for you

Street Light

orderly light
orderly darkness

Memory

oh you
night of reds and greens
with no idea how to torment me

Emotion

jolted awake
to fall in love with silence

Youth

right here
in this place of reproduction and propagation
I was abandoned

岁月

生活向我走来了
从此她就再没有离开过我

诗人

带上自己的心

黎明

但愿我和你怀着同样的心情
去把道路上的黑暗清除干净

白洋淀

别忘了
欢乐的时候
让所有的渔船也在一起碰杯

船

到那个时候
我将和风暴一块回来

Age

life walked toward me
after that she never left me

Poet

bring along your heart

Dawn

if only we had the same desire
to clear all the darkness from the road

Baiyangdian

don't forget
in times of joy
to have all fishing boats clink their glasses, too

Boat

at that point
I will come back with the storm

爱情

即使你离我很远很远
我也一定会记着
是我的
你全都赋予了我

选择

最好
在一个荒芜的地方
安顿我的生活
那时
我将欢迎所有的庄稼
来到我的田野

遗嘱

不论我是怎样的姓名
希望
把她留在这块亲爱的土地上

Love

even if you go far, far away from me
I will still remember
what's mine
all you bestowed upon me

Choice

hopefully
I'll settle down
in some desolate spot
where
I can welcome all the crops
onto my field

Last Will

no matter what my name is
I hope
to leave her on this dear land

街

我至今不清楚自己准确的年龄大概已活了十几年
可是我却知道我的脑袋什么乌七八糟的事都想
我走在街上双脚使劲儿地踩着一个女孩儿的影子
从我身旁晃悠着走过一个被拍着屁股的婴儿睡着了
离我不远的那个老头儿不知他从地下捡走了什么
谁也不理睬那些孩子们挺着肚皮在大街上撒尿
我突然被吓了一跳竟有人把狗放出家门我急忙躲开
人群中不知是什么人在众目睽睽之下呕吐一地
我视而不见转身发现对面一双大胆而放荡的眼睛
我简直不明白她为何这副模样她为什么要出来丢脸
迎面一个无事可干的男人胖得油亮直眉瞪眼地盯着我
我猜不出他想干什么他肚子里打着什么主意
真是讨厌一只挨了打的猫冲着一个呆子叫个没完
我对着它指手画脚地嚷嚷你怎么不蹿上去抓他的脸
可是这个笨蛋反倒逃跑了我诅咒它决不会有好下场
在高处有扇窗户打开着并且跳出一个丑姑娘的面孔
我同她打个招呼闹着玩儿却把她的头吓得缩了进去
我真想不出她想的是什么我感到好笑又觉得无聊
忽然一个女人惊惶的声音像急救车一样尖叫着跑过
紧跟着在她后面传来一个凶恶的男人满嘴的脏话
看热闹的人议论纷纷当中还有人比划着下流手势
一个小伙子把痰吐在了那个画在墙上的女人的身上
我差点儿摔了一跤真他妈的居然路上堆着垃圾
那一头碰在我背后的乞丐他双脚在地面仔细地寻找
这会儿看来已到了晚饭时间只见有钱的走进了饭馆

Street

even today I'm unsure of my actual age I've probably been alive a decade or so
but I know in my mind I'm always thinking about anything and everything
I walk down the street both feet trying to step into some girl's shadow
right beside me a sleeping baby comes rolling by being patted on its butt
far away this old guy plucks up I don't know what from the ground
nobody's paying any attention to those kids bellies out pissing on the street
all of a sudden something scares me someone let a dog out I jump
I don't know who is puking all over in a crowd of staring eyes
I don't see anything so I turn around and find a pair of bold and licentious eyes
I can't figure out why she looks like she would come out to humiliate herself
right before me is an oily-fat man with nothing to do staring at me scowling
I have no idea what he wants to do what plans he's making in that little mind of his
so annoying this cat looking for a beating comes running out hissing nonstop at
       some moron
I point and shout why don't you just jump up and scratch his face
but that little idiot just runs away I curse it nothing good will come
up above a window opens out pops some girl's ugly face
just for fun I wave to her and scare her little head back inside
I can't figure out what she's thinking I found it funny but also pointless
suddenly a woman runs by screaming her head off sounding like an ambulance
chasing right behind her is a vicious looking guy spewing a mouthful of bad words
a crowd of people gathers around making comments and dirty gestures
a kid spits on the body of a girl painted on the wall
I just about trip over a damn pile of trash right there on the street
the beggar whose head hits me in the back is searching the ground with his feet
looks like it's time for dinner only people with money head into restaurants
and an oily-haired ruddy-faced guy is unbuckling his belt scurrying into the
       restroom

而一个油头粉面的家伙却急忙解着裤带钻进厕所
街上的人开始渐渐稀少我注意到他们都回家了
就连那个太阳也好像有家似的它这时也匆匆溜走
天黑了下来我仍旧在街上游荡感到肠胃一阵疼痛
我现在真想发疯似的喊叫让满街都响起我的叫声

the people on the street thin out I notice they're all heading home
even the sun seems to have a home at this point slipping away
the sky's gone dark I'm still hanging out on the street I feel a pain in my stomach
right now I want to scream like a madman the whole street will resound with
      my screams

我是风

北方的树林
落叶纷纷
北方的家园
一片丰收的情景

听，都是孩子
那里遍地都是孩子

一溜烟跑过去的孩子
给母亲带去欢乐的孩子

看，那是辆马车
看看吧
那是拉满了庄稼和阳光的田野
北方的树林
落叶纷纷
我每到这里就来和你幽会
请听我说
我是风

和田野里劳动的孩子一样
我非常热爱天空
当辉煌的太阳一出来
那是母亲睁开的眼睛

I Am Wind

1

northern forest
fallen leaves flying
northern homeland
a harvest scene

listen, it's children
there are children all around

children running off in a puff of smoke
children bringing joy to their mothers

look, there is a horse cart
look further
a field full of crops and sunlight
northern forest
fallen leaves flying
each time I come here we meet in secret
please let me speak
I am wind

2

like the children laboring in the fields
I love the sky
as soon as the glorious sun appears
it is mother's open eye

和田野里劳动的孩子一样
我非常热爱天空
热爱母亲

啊，北方的树林
我对你恋恋不舍
但母亲在召唤
我要和她一起去收割

3

道路飘向远方
抬头看见
那孤零零的头巾下面掠过一道目光

落叶飘扬
侧耳听见
那落叶中发出了告别的喧响

啊，北方的树林
我的美丽的情人
远去的风
在向你歌唱

like the children laboring in the fields
I love the sky
and love mother

northern forest
I cannot give you up
but mother is calling
I must go with her to harvest

3

the road drifts into the distance
look up and see
a gaze beneath the solitary headscarf

fallen leaves drifting
listen closely
the leaves rustle with the noise of separation

northern forest
my beautiful lover
the long traveling wind
is singing to you

荒野

我遍体鳞伤
躺在黎明时的北方
只觉得
一条条金色的河水
像一道道止不住血的伤口
在我身上
静静地流淌

只有云层
把它野性的面孔
朝我挨近
我感觉到了
她那乡土的气息
和带着汗味的肉体
只有云层纠缠着我
我用力地挣脱着
你走开吧
让我独自留在这里

面对着发黑的天际
一个红色的身影渐渐远去
一个白色的身影又向我走来
牵着微风颤栗的小手
她把一块月光的白布
蒙在我的脸上

Wilderness

I'm wounded all over
lying in the north at dawn
feeling nothing but
golden rivers
like the wounds on my body
bleeding nonstop
a silent flow

only the stratosphere
brings its untamed face
toward me
I can feel
her pastoral breath
and sweaty physique
only the stratosphere entangles me
I struggle to get free
get off
leave me alone

facing a darkening horizon
one red shadow grows distant
while a white shadow's coming closer
with the white cloth of moonlight
quivering in her tiny hand
she covers my face

蒙住了我的眼睛
蒙住了我的呻吟
可是我的心
却高举在手中
她是一束鲜花
她是一束光明

我多么希望
把这鲜花和光明
连同我的名字和眼睛
一块儿都刻进自己的碑文
我多么想看到
明天或将来
那到这里来开垦
和来为我哀悼的人们

she covers my eyes
she covers my cries
but my heart
she holds high in her hand
she is a bouquet of flowers
she is a bouquet of light

how I wish
these flowers and light
plus my name and my eyes
could be carved into a stele
how I wish to see
tomorrow or some point in the future
the people who'll come here
for cultivation or else to mourn me

阳光

阳光在土地上生长
它把白天的面孔
用它的茎
拱出了地面
而那些同样已撕开
身上泥土的白骨
一个个转动空空的眼窝
他们先是看一眼
头上的天空
又环顾一下
四周拥挤的花枝
然后，他们便急匆匆地
各自朝自己所思念的地方
爬去……

阳光在土地上生长
阳光——
那中间又乱哄哄地走来了
一群刚刚逃离黑暗的人们

Sunlight

sunlight grows on the earth
it takes the face of day
and pushes up through the ground
with its stalk
and those bones that also have
pushed soil off their selves
first they look at
the sky overhead
with their rolling empty eye sockets
then look around
at the crowding flora
then rush
crawling back to wherever
each longs for . . .

sunlight grows on the earth
sunlight—
and amidst it a horde of
people recently escaped from darkness

黄昏

这时已听不到
太阳有力的爪子
在地上行走
这时是昏暗的
这时正是黄昏
这时的黄昏就象是一张
已被剥下来的
已被风干的兽皮一样

但这时的人们
我在路上遇到他们
他们仍警觉地注视着
四周的一切动静
这使我也变得小心
在这黄昏之后
还会不会出现
比这更凶猛的野兽的眼睛

Dusk

now no more can be heard
the sun's powerful claws
strolling the earth
now is a gloominess
now it is dusk
the dusk now like a
a skinned
wind-dried animal pelt

but the people now
seen on the street
keep staring fiercely
at every movement
keeping me guarded
after dusk
will the eyes of an even
more vicious beast appear

雪地上的夜

雪地上的夜
是一只长着黑白毛色的狗
月亮是它时而伸出的舌头
星星是它时而露出的牙齿

就是这只狗
这只被冬天放出来的狗
这只警惕地围着我们房屋转悠的狗
正用北风的
那常常使人从安睡中惊醒的声音
冲着我们嚎叫

这使我不得不推开门
愤怒地朝它走去
这使我不得不对着黑夜怒斥
你快点儿从这里滚开吧

可是黑夜并没有因此而离去
这只雪地上的狗
照样在外面转悠
当然，它的叫声也一直持续了很久
直到我由于疲惫不知不觉地睡去
并梦见眼前已是春暖花开的时候

Night on the Snow-covered Ground

on the snow-covered ground night
is a dog with black and white fur
the moon is the tongue it sticks out
the stars are the teeth it bares

it's this dog
this dog set loose by winter
this dog vigilantly pacing around our home
shouting at us
with the northern wind
that jolts us from our peaceful sleep

leaving me no choice but to push past the door
and rush up to it in anger
leaving me no choice but to denounce the night
you better get out of here in a hurry

but the night never goes away
on the snow-covered ground the dog
is still out there pacing
and of course its shouts keep on
beyond falling asleep, exhausted
to dream of spring flowers blooming before my eyes

如今的日子

如今的日子
更显得虚弱和怯懦
它就像一个
不久刚受过侮辱和折磨的人
你看它走在街上躲躲闪闪
它或许永远也不会忘掉
一个好端端的白天
是怎样在日落的时候
被一只伸过来的大手
凶狠地抓住头发拽走

如今的日子
更显得虚弱和怯懦
它同街上的
那剽悍而又灵活的寒冷
形成鲜明的对照
你看寒冷在人群中
是多么肆无忌惮
而你呢？即使你所碰到的风
并不是什么强有力的对手
看样子你也会被它一拳击倒

A Day Like Today

a day like today
seems even more weak and timid
like someone
who's just been insulted and tormented
you see it on the street ducking and diving
perhaps it will never forget
how a day so shiny and bright
had been dragged cruelly away by the hair
by a great outstretched hand
when the sun went down

a day like today
seems even weaker and more timid
against the agile and lithe
cold on the street
it forms a clear contrast
you can see how unscrupulous
the cold is in a crowd
but you? even if the wind you came across
were not so powerful an opponent
you'd still get knocked down in one punch

阳光中的向日葵

你看到了吗
你看到阳光中的那棵向日葵了吗
你看它，它没有低下头
而是把头转向身后
就好象是为了一口咬断
那套在它脖子上的
那牵在太阳手中的绳索

你看到它了吗
你看到那棵昂着头
怒视着太阳的向日葵了吗
它的头几乎已把太阳遮住
它的头即使是在没有太阳的时候
也依然在闪耀着光芒

你看到那棵向日葵了吗
你应该走近它
你走近它便会发现
它脚下的那片泥土
每抓起一把
都一定会攥出血来

Sunflower in the Sun

do you see
do you see that sunflower in the sun
you see, it doesn't bow its head
but turns it back
it turns its head
as if to bite through
the rope around its neck
held by the sun's hands

do you see it
do you see that sunflower, raising its head
glaring at the sun
its head almost eclipses the sun
yet even with no sun
its head still glows

do you see that sunflower
you should get closer
get close and you'll find
the soil beneath its feet
each handful of soil
oozes blood

translated by Huang Yibing and Jonathan Stalling

老房子

那屋顶
那破旧的帽子
它已戴了很多年
虽然那顶帽子
也曾被风的刷子刷过
也曾被雨水洗过
但最终还是从污垢里钻出了草
它每日坐在街旁
它从不对谁说什么
它只是用它那使人揣摩不透的眼神
看着过往的行人
它面无光泽
它神情忧伤
那是因为它常常听到
它的那些儿女
总是对它不满地唠叨

Old House

the roof
an old tattered hat
has been worn so many years
that even though this hat
was blown off by a brush of wind
and washed by the rain
in the end grass still pierces through the filth
each day it sits by the street
never speaking to anyone
just staring at pedestrians
with its unfathomable eyes
no luster in its face
only distress in its expression
because it still hears
its sons and daughters
and all their gripes

灯

灯突然亮了
只见灯光的利爪
踩着醉汉们冷冰冰的脸
灯，扑打着巨大的翅膀
这使我惊愕地看见
在它的巨大的翅膀下面
那些像是死了的眼睛
正向外流着酒……

灯突然亮了
这灯光引起了一阵骚乱
你听醉汉们大声嚷嚷
它是从哪儿飞来的
我们为什么还不把它赶走
我们为什么要让它来啄食我们
我们宁愿在黑暗中死……

灯突然亮了
只听灯下有人小声地问我
你说这灯是让它亮着呢
还是应该把它关掉

Lamp

suddenly the lamp turns on
I only see the sharp claws of the light
stomping on the cold faces of drunks
the lamp, beating its great wings
shows me in shock
beneath its great wings
wine flows forth
from what look like dead eyes . . .

suddenly the lamp turns on
the light creates a disturbance
I hear the shouts of drunks
where'd it fly in from
why don't we get rid of it
why do we let it eat off us
we'd rather die in the dark . . .

suddenly the lamp turns on
I hear only someone's whispered question
you think this lamp should stay on
or be turned off

一夜之后

轻轻地打开门
你让那搂着你
睡了一宿的夜走出去
你看见它的背影很快消失
你开始听到
黎明的车轮
又在街上发出响声
你把窗户推开
你把关了一屋子的梦
全都轰到空中
你把昨晚欢乐抖落的羽毛
打扫干净
随后，你对着镜子打量自己
你看见自己的两只眼睛
都独自浮动在自己的眼眶里
那样子简直就像
两条交配之后
便各自游走的鱼……

One Night Later

softly opening the door
you let out the night
that held you sleeping in its arms
you see its shadow quickly disappear
you begin to hear
the dawn's wheels
make their noises on the street again
you push the window open
you chase the locked-in dreams
out into the air
you sweep up
the feathers happily shaken to the ground
then size yourself up in the mirror
looking at your eyes
hovering in their sockets
looking like nothing but
two fish swimming off
after spawning . . .

昨天与今天

昨天——
它什么也没有留下
它把该带走的全都带走了
而今天
你又是怎样的呢
你也许正将门仔细地关好
你也许正忙于捕捉
那飞来飞去的
但最后还是落在床上的嘴唇
你也许正不耐烦地等待着
那将会被端到你面前的
那迟迟还没有端来的
熟透了的乳房
你也许正迅速地
替别人解开衣服
如同打开一扇窗户
但你却发现
你无法看清里面
就好像
那是一间阴暗而又空荡的屋子
你也许已养成了贪睡的习惯
你也许正要躺下
可你只要躺下
很快就会梦见自己变了
变得连自己也不认识
你总觉得
你是被埋葬在什么地方

80

Yesterday and Today

yesterday—
it left nothing
everything it should have taken it took
but today
well how will you be
maybe you will cautiously lock the door
maybe you are busy trying to catch
the lips that fly around
always to land on the bed in the end
maybe you are patiently waiting
for the arrival of those
ripe breasts which never arrive
before your face
maybe you are quickly
taking your clothes off for someone
like opening a window
only to discover
you can't see inside
as if it were some
dark and deserted room
maybe you've developed a habit of drowsiness
maybe you're lying down
but as soon as you do
you start dreaming of change
changing so you don't recognize yourself
and you feel
you've been buried somewhere

身体已在腐烂
并还覆盖着一层苔藓
要么，你也许就是昏沉沉的
整日如此
你这会儿或许又喝足了酒
脑子里便开始反复出现
一段模糊的人体
也许，你此时已进入梦幻
你就觉得自己的头
仿佛被一棵疯了的树
一把抓起
并且在空中用力地摇晃
或者，你感到你的心轻飘飘的
像红色的气球一样
朝着天空飞去
你自认为它赶走了太阳
而且已占据太阳的位置
或许，你现在正走在街上
把脸揭下来
你把脸撕得粉碎
随后，扔得满街都是
也许，这都是可能的
完全可能的
你这时突然遭到不幸
你这时在忍受痛苦
你这时仍旧一无所获
你这时已面临绝境
或者，你这时的处境
根本就不由自己
你只好任凭时间在捉弄你
在拽长你的胡子……

your body decomposing
and covered in moss
or, maybe you're befuddled
all day long you feel it
perhaps you've been drinking
and someone's unclear shape
sticks in your mind
and maybe you've slipped into a dream
and you feel your own head
being carried off and
shaken in the sky by
a tree gone mad
or else, you feel your heart go light
like a red balloon
flying into the air
you think it's pushed the sun aside
to occupy its place
or perhaps, you're walking down the street
pulling off your face
and tearing it to shreds
and scattering it over the ground
maybe, it's all possible
absolutely possible
right now you encounter misfortune
right now you tolerate pain
right now you've gained nothing
right now you face an impasse
or else, right now your predicament
is not your own
you'd better leave it to time to embarrass you
to pull down your beard . . .

好啦，我想再最后说一句
我想我不知为什么会这样想
今天——
它简直就像一个
野蛮的汉子
一个把你按倒在地
并随意摆布的汉子

okay, I've thought of a final line
I think I don't know why I'm thinking this
today—
it's just like a
wild man
a man who'll knock you to the ground
and order you around without a thought

晚年

墙壁已爬满了皱纹
墙壁就如同一面镜子
一个老人从中看到了一位老人
屋子里静悄悄的，没有钟
听不到嘀嗒声，屋子里
静悄悄的，但是那位老人
他却似乎一直在倾听着什么
也许，人活到了这般年岁
就能够听到——时间
——它就像是个屠夫
在暗地里不停地磨刀子的声音
他似乎一直在倾听着什么
他在听着什么
他到底听到了什么

Late Years

the wall is crawling with wrinkles
the wall is like a mirror
an old man looking at an old man from within
the room is silent, and there is no clock
to tick-tock, the room
is silent, but the old man
seems to be listening in on something
perhaps, reaching this age
you can hear—time
—like a butcher
in the dark ground the endless sound of sharpening knives
he seems to be listening in on something
what's he listening to
what can he hear

死后也还会衰老

地里已长出死者的白发
这使我相信：人死后也还会衰老

人死后也还会有噩梦扑在身上
也还会惊醒，睁眼看到

又一个白天从蛋壳里出世
并且很快便开始忙于在地上啄食

也还会听见自己的脚步
听出自己的双腿在欢笑在忧愁

也还会回忆，尽管头脑里空洞洞的
尽管那些心里的人们已经腐烂

也还会歌颂他们，歌颂爱人
用双手稳稳地接住她的脸

然后又把她小心地放进草丛
看着她笨拙地拖出自己性感的躯体

也还会等待，等待阳光
最后像块破草席一样被风卷走

等待日落，它就如同害怕一只猛兽
会撕碎它的肉似的躲开你

Even After Death We Grow Old

the white hair of the dead grows from the ground
which makes me believe: even after death we grow old

after we die nightmares will still throw themselves on us
and wake us, as we open our eyes to see

another day hatch from its eggshell
to start pecking for food on the ground

we will hear our own footsteps
hear our own feet laughing and worrying

we will remember, even if our brains are empty
even if those in our hearts have already decomposed

we will eulogize them, eulogize our loved ones
gently hold their faces in our hands

and carefully lay them down in the bushes
to watch them clumsily pull their sexy shapes out

we will wait, wait for the sunlight
to be carried by the wind like a tattered straw mat

wait for the sunset, avoiding you as if in fear of
a wild animal tearing through its flesh

而夜晚，它却温顺地让你拉进怀里
任随你玩弄，发泄，一声不吭

也还会由于劳累就地躺下，闭目
听着天上群兽在争斗时发出的吼叫

也还会担忧，或许一夜之间
天空的血将全部流到地上

也还会站起来，哀悼一副死去的面孔
可她的眼睛还在注视着你

也还会希望，愿自己永远地活着
愿自己别是一只被他人猎取的动物

被放进火里烤着，被吞食
也还会痛苦，也还会不堪忍受啊

地里已经长出死者的白发
这使我相信：人死后也还会衰老

and the night, meekly pulling you into its arms
no matter how you fuss, or vent, or make no sound

we will collapse to the ground in exhaustion, eyes closed
listening to the cackle of birds fighting in the sky

we will worry, will the sky's blood
pour onto the earth over night

we will stand, mourning a dead face
though her eyes still stare at you

we will hope, wishing we could live forever
wishing we were not some animal to be hunted

cooked over open flame, eaten
we will hurt, and oh we won't be able to bear it

the white hair of the dead grows from the ground
which makes me believe: even after death we grow old

选自《没有时间的时间》

第一篇：序

这里已不再有感情生长
这里是一片光秃秃的时间
阴暗而又寒冷
寂静而又空荡
这里是一片被灰尘覆盖的时间
不再有记忆，也不再有思想
不再期待，也不再希望
这里曾有过你生活的时间
也曾有过我生活的时间
这里是没有时间的时间

在这里，生和死已不存在界线
我们没有必要去证明我们活着
我们从没有过开始
我们也没有结束
结束的只是应该结束的时间
我们还是我们
我与我也没有区分
我的过去仍旧是我现在的镜子
我的现在是我未来的倒影
在这里，生和死已不存在界线
我没有必要去惧怕死亡

我伴随着我
我了解我
那是因为我是我

from Time Without Time

I: Overture

no more feelings are growing here
here is a blank expanse of time
dark and cold
solitary and empty
it is time covered in dust here
no more memory, no more thought
no more expectations, no more hope
there used to be time you lived in here
and time I lived in
it is timeless time here

there is no more border between life and death here
we have no need to prove we are alive
we have never begun
nor did we end
what ended was time as it should have ended
we are still us
there is no difference between me and I
my past is still the mirror of my present
my present is still the reflection of my future
there is no more border between life and death here
I have no reason to fear death

I follow me
I understand me
because I am me

当你用人的眼睛来看我
我仅仅是另外一个人
只有人会把人当做人
只有人在把人当人看
我可以拥有我们
我也可以失去我们
我可以有我
我也可以无我
我活着需要的是有
而不是没有
没有比没有更能够把我摧毁
我们没有开始
我们也没有结束
我们不是我们的开始
我们也不是我们的结束

这里是一片光秃秃的时间
这里是一片被灰尘覆盖的时间
这里是没有时间的时间

我想，我的出现
不会使你感到意外
正如你的出现一样
也不会令我吃惊
我们不会奇怪我们
我们并不奇怪
我们奇怪的也许是
人与人最根本的区别是没有区别
我们在活着
我们知道我们活着
我们的道理，都是我们的道理

when you see me with human eyes
I am just another human being
only a human being will see a human being as a human being
only a human being taking a human being for a human being
I can own us
as I can lose us
I can have me
as I can be without me
what I need to live is to have
not to be without
nothing will cause us more ruin than nothing
we have no beginning
we have no ending
we are not our beginning
nor are we our ending

it is a blank expanse of time here
it is time covered in dust here
it is time without time here

I think that my appearance
won't seem accidental
any more than your appearance
and will not surprise me
we won't be curious about us
we are not curious
what we might be curious about is that
the fundamental distinction between human beings is no distinction
we are alive
we know we are alive
our reasons are our reasons

我就是我的道理
看，我们如今又一次出现
来到这里，庄重而又坦荡
可是我的思绪
却好似一场大雪纷纷扬扬
我感觉我在这里
全身渐渐变得洁白
我发现我已不再是我
我一点儿都不肮脏

I am my reason
look, we reappear now
and come here, dignified and magnanimous
but my mind
stirs like a snowstorm
I feel myself here
body gradually turning white
finding I am no longer me
I am spotless

第二篇

1

大风从岩石上刮过
磨快它的刀口
只听轰隆一声
黑夜沉重地倒下
只见那个庞然大物被剥掉了皮
又被一刀剖开腹部
随后，便有一团鲜红的肉
滚了出来……
太阳诞生了
可阳光却已经苍老
它拄着拐杖在地上走

2

我这是刚刚从梦的水里爬上岸
我身上湿淋淋、浑身无力
你说，我们今天应该去做什么
我还想睡一会儿、再睡一会儿
就让我们的尾巴紧紧地缠绕在一起
我身上湿淋淋，浑身无力
你这个总是打呼噜的
雷的儿子，你可梦见
那海里的琴了吗
那琴声是多么悠扬，多么悦耳

II

1

the wind blows off the cliff
quickening its blade
a rumbling sound
and the night collapses under its weight
seeing only that colossus stripped of skin
and eviscerated with a knife
as afterward burgundy flesh
rolls out . . .
the sun is born
yet sunlight is so aged
it walks along on a cane

2

I have just climbed ashore from the waters of a dream
my body spent and wet
you say, what should we do today
I want to keep sleeping, go back to sleep
and for our tails to entwine
my body spent and wet
you the constantly snoring
son of thunder, were you dreaming of
the zither in the ocean
its tone so mellifluous, melodious

我还想睡一会儿，再睡一会儿
你不要对着我
张大肚脐的嘴巴
瞪大乳房的眼

3

（一对懒惰的夫妇
他们光着身子，不冷也不热
他们的眼里混浊）
你们睁开眼睛是白天
你们闭上眼睛是黑夜
堕落的汉子
放荡的妇人
小心你们身后的大棒
你们可听说过
那好色的河水可得到了报应
就是因为好色
它被弄瞎了一只眼

4

你看我这身上多瘦呵
你脱掉羽毛变成女人
我总想躲开你
我总是躲不开你
我这是在害怕
害怕你有四张脸
害怕你的秃头
害怕你的酷热

I want to keep sleeping, go back to sleep
do not open that great navel of your mouth
toward me
and stare with the grand breasts of your eyes

3

(a lazy husband and wife
naked, neither cold nor hot
murkiness in their eyes)
opening your eyes it is day
shutting your eyes night
a fallen man
an unfaithful wife
beware the club behind you
maybe you've heard of it
the lascivious river met its retribution
because it was lascivious
it was blinded in one eye

4

look how skinny I am
pluck all your feathers and turn into a woman
I try to avoid you
But never can
this is my fear
afraid of your four faces
afraid of your bald head
afraid of your scorching heat

我总想躲开你
我总是躲不开你
我就好像看见无数的飞虫
搅得天昏地暗
为此,我想
我应该剪一缕头发送给你
我是让你受我欺骗
我是在让你为我而死

5

一夜的温柔
你可怀了孕
但愿你不要生出别的东西
一夜过去了,我没有睡好
我总是听见
那离我还远的地方有棵树
在不时地发出嘶叫
像是有谁骑在了它的背上
像是有谁抓住了它的鬃毛
一夜过去了,我没有睡好
我一会儿想起你们
我一会儿又忘记你们
头脑里漆黑一片
记忆深如水井
我投下一个石子
只能传来一下回声

I try to avoid you
but never can
like seeing a swarm of insects
covering the earth and blackening the sky
for this, I think
I should give you a lock of my hair
I make you take my lies
I make you die for me

5

the tenderness of a night
and you're pregnant
so long as you don't give birth to anything else
a night has passed, I didn't sleep well
always hearing
that tree so far away from me
whining intermittently
like someone were riding its back
like someone were pulling its mane
a night has passed, I didn't sleep well
thinking of you
and then forgetting you
all blackness in my head
memory deep as a well
I throw in a pebble
only an echo can return

6

我们是泥土的肉
我们是肉的泥土
我们从昨天又来到今天
今天，我不想让你
用你的花园来吻我
我也不想去摘
你身上的桃子
我不想，我什么也不想
我低着头，像秋天饱满的谷穗
只等着被刈割
我不想，我什么也不想
我有的仅仅是无有
我没有的却是所有

7

我们像土地一样
没有失去生殖的能力
我会把生命注入你的身体
别看我已白发丛生
可是我还没老到
成为一块石头
我还会对你说
别用黑暗把自己紧裹着
别去昏睡
我需要的不是吃你的奶
而是需要吸足你的爱
并为此而陶醉
荡漾在你光明的皮肤上

6

we are flesh of mud
we are mud of flesh
we arrive again at today from yesterday
today, I don't want you to
kiss me with your garden
and I don't want to pick
peaches from your body
I don't want it, I don't want anything
I bow my head, like the full grains of autumn
waiting to be mowed down
I don't want it, I don't want anything
all I have is nothing
what I do not have is everything

7

we are like the earth
no ability to stop reproducing
I will plant life inside you
ignore my grey hair
I'm not so old I can't
become a stone
I can still say to you
do not wrap yourself in darkness
do not give in to lethargy
I don't need to drink your milk
but to ingest your love
and get drunk on it
rippling over your bright skin

8

在一片寂静中是寂静
在一个男人的火焰中
一个女人像是一锅烧开的水
有人在哈哈大笑
而我却又被抓进梦的牢笼
我只好在梦中想象
我只好在梦中苏醒
在一片寂静中是寂静
在我黑色的梦里
不知是谁在发出绝望的喊叫
这声音似长矛把我刺穿
而我却流不出血
我没有血
我躯体透明
我没有颜色

8

in silence is silence
in a man's flame
a woman is like a pot of boiling water
someone laughs
but again I am caught in dream's cage
I must imagine in a dream
I must wake in a dream
in silence is silence
in my black dream
who is it screaming in desperation
its sound piercing through me like a spear
but I do not bleed
I have no blood
my body is translucent
I am colorless

第五篇

当我看见阳光
像一群蜜蜂爬满你的头顶
你这时已昏昏欲睡
我想起身离开你
但是我没能站起来
我的双腿已不听我使唤
我的两脚还在鞋里呼呼大睡
我身体的其它部位
这会儿也开始骚动
我根本无法控制自己
我已经不再听从我的指挥
我想喊叫
我发不出声音
我急得想哭
我流不出眼泪
我想痛打自己
我握不了拳头，也挥不动手臂
我想发脾气，可是我没脾气
我只好老老实实，一动不动
任凭眼珠在得意地东瞧西看
任凭头脑在发疯地胡思乱想
任凭身体在任意地胡作非为
任凭自己在戏弄自己
我骂我
我反过来骂我
我嘲笑我
我反唇相讥
我不搭理我
我只得不搭理我

V

when I see the sunlight
overrun your head like a swarm of bees
you are falling asleep
I want to get up and leave you
but cannot stand
my legs no longer listen to my command
my feet still asleep in their shoes
the rest of my body
is only starting to stir
I have no way to control myself
but no longer follow my orders
I want to scream
but cannot make a sound
I feel like crying
but cannot shed tears
I want to hit myself
but cannot make a fist, or swing my arms
I want to lose my temper, but have no temper
I might as well be calm, unmoving
smugly looking around with my eyes
free-associating with my brain
thrashing randomly with my body
toying myself with myself
I curse myself
I curse myself back
I laugh at myself
I deride myself
I ignore myself
I can only ignore myself

我抛弃我
我被我抛弃
我现在自己已不再属于自己
我无法控制我
这似乎不足为奇
就连我想去死都死不了
因为我已对我没有权力

当我看见阳光
像一群蜜蜂爬满你的头顶
这已不是我看见阳光
像一群蜜蜂爬满你的头顶
我见你昏昏欲睡
这已不是我见你昏昏欲睡
我想起身离开你
这已不是我想起身离开你
我没能站起来
我已不是我没能站起来
不是，你听着
绝对不是

I abandon myself
and am abandoned by myself
I no longer belong to myself
but cannot control myself
nothing surprising about that
even if I wanted to die I couldn't
having no power over myself

when I see the sunlight
overrun your head like a swarm of bees
it's not me seeing the sunlight
overrun your head like a swarm of bees
my seeing you falling asleep
is not me seeing you fall asleep
my wanting to get up and leave you
is not my wanting to get up and leave you
my not being able to stand
is not my inability to stand
no, listen
it isn't

第九篇

我醒后，屋内静悄悄
我听得见你心脏的钟表
在嘀嗒地走
天还没亮
离天亮不知还有多久
我望不到夜的尽头
我醒后，想到时间
想到我们是在时间的深处
想到我们也是时间
我们就像海水在漆黑的海洋里一样
我们是时间中的时间

我们是飘动的时间
但不知飘向何方
我已不能辨别
我们所在的位置
也不能辨别方向
我们是飘动的时间
所有的方向都是一个方向
所有的方向都是我们的去向
我们向前
也是在后退
我们的运动
也是静止
我们就像是沙粒
在无边的荒漠上
我们是时间中的时间

IX

I wake, the room silent
I hear the clock of your heart
ticking on
not yet light out
I don't know when it will be light
not that I'm looking for the end of night
I wake, thinking of time
thinking we are in the depths of time
thinking that we too are time
we are like seawater in the black sea
we are time within time

we are drifting time
without knowing where we're drifting
I can no longer tell
our position
nor our direction
we are drifting time
all directions one direction
all directions our destination
what is ahead
is what is behind
our motion
is our stasis
we are sand
in a boundless desert
we are time within time

你心脏的钟表
还在嘀嗒地走着
你心脏的时间已是什么时间
我不知道
但我却能从你的脸上看出
那钟表的指针
在你的身体上走动
就像牛在拉着犁一样
你已有了皱纹
你在急促地呼吸
你嘴里传出的声音持久而又单调
你一定会有所感受
你所感受的是你的感受
你心脏的时间已是什么时间
我不知道
我只听见你心脏的钟表
还在嘀嗒地走
还在黑暗中走
我们是时间中的时间

天还没有亮
我不知离天亮还有多久
黑夜如此辽阔
我不知距白天还有多远
我们是在时间的深处
我们也是时间
我们现在是黑色的时间
我醒后，屋内静悄悄
你心脏的钟表在嘀嗒地走

the clock of your heart
is still ticking on
what time the time of your heart is
I do not know
but I can tell from your face
the hands of the clock
move over your body
like an ox pulling a plow
you have wrinkles
your breathing is rushed
the sound from your mouth is protracted yet monotone
you must be able to feel it
what you feel is your feeling
what time the time of your heart is
I do not know
I only hear the clock of your heart
ticking on
in the darkness
we are time within time

it's not yet light out
I don't know when it will be light
the night is so vast
I don't know when it will be day
we are in the depths of time
and we are time
right now we are a black time
I wake, the room silent
the clock of your heart ticking on

第十三篇

1

我头脑里的果实已挂满枝头
秋风又一次踏上我心中的田野
那里也从一片绿色变成一片金黄
如今，我已经步入
自己的另一个季节
我是用衰老换来的收获

2

想起过去
我们曾一起播种爱情
你那时浑身的泥土都在沸腾
我时常在你之上
为你落下阵阵春雨
雨水滋润着我们的幸福

3

有多少个夜晚
我的眼睛把你照耀
你的皮肤一片银白
尽管狂风似狼群
在窗外嚎叫
也不曾引起我们的胆怯
有多少个夜晚
你让我闻到你身上的花香
你让我看到
你嘴唇的花朵在月光中开放

XIII

1

the fruits in my mind fill the branches
the autumn wind again steps onto the field in my heart
where it goes golden from green
and now, I step into
another of the self's seasons
with harvest traded in for old age

2

thinking of the past
and our sowing of love
how your mud-covered body seethed
I was often above you
raining down spring showers on you
to moisten our happiness

3

how many nights
did my eyes illuminate you
your skin silver
even a pack of wolves
howling outside our window
never caused us to cower
how many nights
did I smell your fragrance
did I see
the flower of your lips bloom in the moonlight

4

我常常感到
我就像是一只船
漂荡在你的水面
船身摇晃
打破了你的平静
而你掀起波浪
撞击着我的船舷
我的四周簇拥着浪花
我如同置身于花园里一样
我置身于你的怀抱

5

可美好的日子
却也曾被劈成碎块
我们有离合，也有悲欢
我记得那时
人不让做人，人在做鬼
你生在地上却求得是天
你有嘴却不能说话
你有眼却不能看
你有腿却不能走路
你有情也只能无情
我们每天只好用心去生活
但尽管这样，我们偶尔相遇
我也能看得懂你脸上的万语千言

4

I often feel
like a boat
floating on your water
a boat whose rocking
breaks your calm
your ripples
strike my gunwales
whitecaps cluster around me
placing me in a garden
placing me in your arms

5

what a beautiful day
split to shreds
we have our vicissitudes, our divisions and reunions
I remember when
we were demons, not allowed to be ourselves
you were born on the earth to long for the sky
you had a mouth but not to speak with
you had eyes but not to see with
you had feet but not to walk with
you had passion but could only be dispassionate
we can only live our lives with our hearts
yet even so, when we happen to meet
I can read your face's thousands of words

6

人们涌向希望的门口
人们在希望的大门进进出出
我记得那天我在门外等你
你终于出来了
你的青春十分瘦弱
我们同路，我们并排走
我们虽然抛弃了希望
可我们并不绝望

7

我们送走了一个个死去的日子
那一个个死去的日子
已埋进土里，渐渐变成白骨
我们也曾为我们失去每一天
和失去阳光而伤过心
我们的眼里
流过泪也流过血
但我们并不乞求
乞求我们不老和不死
我们只愿自己活着像个人

8

你一度曾长满新芽
你一度曾枝叶茂盛
你一度曾满身枯叶
又被大风一扫而光
你的一生就如同起伏的浪涛

6

people pour toward hope's gates
go in and out the gates of hope
I remember that day waiting for you outside the gate
the complete frailness of your youth
when you finally appeared
on the same path, we walked side by side
though we gave up hope
we did not despair

7

we have sent off day after dead day
buried in the ground
each dead day becomes bones
for the sake of us we lost every day
and been hurt by the loss of the sun
our eyes
have shed both tears and blood
but we do not beg
beg that we do not age or die
we only wish to live like ourselves

8

once you were covered in new growth
once you were flush with foliage
once your body was covered in withered leaves
and then blown bare by the wind
your life was like the surging of surf

你不是居浪峰之上
便是落于浪谷之中
但你一直是自己最忠实的守护者
你也将永远是你的爱人

if you do not live at the peak of the wave
then you live in its valley
but you are always your own most loyal protector
you will always be your own lover

第十六篇

在这块曾掩埋过无数死者的地方
如今又长出绿油油的日子
一座老房子的墙皮已经剥落
我也不再是从前的我
在今天人们的眼里
我是老朽，像化石
我的时间似乎不再流动血液
我现在已被现在遗弃
我的过去也已被现在遗忘
我每天只有自己守候着自己
自己牵着自己的影子
我落满灰尘

我的生命也似乎不再是生命
我的历史无人翻阅
我也不再翻阅自己
我不想自己再看到自己
我就是这样地在等待自己腐烂
我慢慢地在腐烂
我不死，可也不像在活着
我已不再是从前的我
我已没有笑容
我也不会再笑
即使我偶尔把嘴咧开
也显得那么丑陋
我现在已不会像过去似的
来把人吸引
吸引人来采摘我的微笑
我已没有笑容
我满脸冷清

XVI

in this land that has buried countless dead
a new green day is now born
an old home's façade is taken down
I am no longer the me I once was
in people's eyes today
I'm ancient, like a fossil
as if no blood flowed through my time
I am discarded by the now
the now forgets my past
only I keep wait for myself every day
holding onto my own shadow
covered in dust

as if my life were life no more
nobody reads through my history
not that I read through myself
I don't want to see myself
this is me waiting for myself to decompose
I am decomposing slowly
not dying, but not living either
I am no longer the me I once was
I have no more smile
and will not laugh again
even if I happen to open my mouth
it wouldn't look very good
I can't be like I used to be
drawing people in
drawing people in to pluck my smile
I have no more smile
my face a cold blank

我的两眼无神就像两片枯叶
在从高处飘落
飘落在地上
渐渐变得污浊

这人世间依然还有一小块地方
摆着我这颗无用的头
我的躯体，像只破船
却还没有沉没
我每日照旧浸泡在
茫茫人生的水流里
只是我的生活已不是生活
我的头脑早已空空如也
没有过去，也没有现在
更不能去想象将来
我的心中也已荒无人烟
越来越阴森可怖
我的心比我还要孤独
我现在真像一座坟墓
自己埋葬自己
但我还是怕死
我也怕活着

在这块曾掩埋过无数死者的地方
如今又长出绿油油的日子
一座老房子的墙皮已经剥落
我也不再是从前的我
我的记忆里已没有记忆
我的记忆里空空荡荡
即使还残留着一点儿东西
也已模糊不清

my eyes lifeless like wilted leaves
fluttering down
fluttering onto the ground
and slowly rotting there

there is still a place in this human world
to put this useless head of mine
my body, like an old boat
has not sunk
every day I soak it
in the expanses of the river of life
but my life is no life
my mind has long been empty
with no past, no present
not to mention any future
and no signs of life in my heart
danker and more horrid by the day
it's lonelier than I am
I am quite like a grave
In which to bury myself
yet still fearing death
just as I'm afraid of life

in this land that has buried countless dead
a new green day is now born
an old home's façade is taken down
I am no longer the me I once was
my memories have no memories
they are an emptiness
it is unclear
if anything remains

我不再痛苦，也不再幸福
我不再会为了我的幸福而痛苦
我即将结束
把一切抛弃
我现在已被我挥霍干净
我梦的大门不再打开
我思想的墓穴开始封闭
我在同我告别
我不留恋
我同我分手之后将一无所有
我在结束
结束的是我
死亡从我的身上什么也不会得到

I have neither pain nor pleasure
my pleasure will give me no more pain
I am about to end
to abandon it all
I have been squandered clean
the gate of my dreams will not reopen
the tomb of my thoughts is starting to close
I say goodbye to myself
without reluctance
after departing from myself I will have nothing
I am ending
what is ending is myself
death will get nothing from me

Translator Biographies

Lucas Klein is a father, writer, translator and editor whose work has appeared in *Jacket*, *Rain Taxi*, *CLEAR*, and *PMLA*, and from Fordham, Black Widow, and New Directions. Assistant Professor at the University of Hong Kong, his translation *Notes on the Mosquito: Selected Poems of Xi Chuan* won the 2013 Lucien Stryk Prize. He is translating Tang dynasty poet Li Shangyin.

Huang Yibing (Mai Mang) is a Chinese poet and Associate Professor of Chinese at Connecticut College. He received his PhD in Chinese literature from Beijing University and a second PhD in comparative literature from UCLA. He is the author of *Contemporary Chinese Literature: From the Cultural Revolution to the Future* (New York: Palgrave Macmillan, 2007) and two books of poetry, *Stone Turtle: Poems 1987–2000* (2005) and *Approaching Blindness* (2005).

Jonathan Stalling is Professor of English at the University of Oklahoma where he also serves as the Curator of the Chinese Literature Translation Archive and as the Editor of the *Chinese Literature Today* magazine and book series. Stalling is the author of several books including *Poetics of Emptiness*, *Yingelishi*, and *Lost Wax: Translation through the Void*. He is also the translator of *Winter Sun: The Poetry of Shi Zhi*.

JINTIAN SERIES OF CONTEMPORARY LITERATURE

Flash Cards
Yu Jian
Translated by Wang Ping & Ron Padgett

The Changing Room
Zhai Yongming
Translated by Andrea Lingenfelter

Doubled Shadows
Ouyang Jianghe
Translated by Austin Woerner

A Phone Call from Dalian
Han Dong
Edited by Nicky Harman
Translated by Nicky Harman, Maghiel van Crevel,
Yu Yan Chen, Naikan Tao, Tony Prince & Michael Day

Wind Says
Bai Hua
Translated by Fiona Sze-Lorrain

I Can Almost See the Clouds of Dust
Yu Xiang
Translated by Fiona Sze-Lorrain

Canyon in the Body
Lan Lan
Translated by Fiona Sze-Lorrain

Something Crosses My Mind
Wang Xiaoni
Translated by Eleanor Goodman